LE PETIT PARIS

FRENCH FINGER FOOD

NATHALIE BENEZET

CONTENTS

INTRODUCTION

Paris is a beautiful, inspiring city, and I have spent much of my life there. French people have a true passion for cooking, and the cuisine is a natural part of the culture. It is as much about the quality of the products and the preparation of the meals as it is about eating.

When I moved to London the one thing I missed was the food back home – in particular the wonderful delicacies sold in the brasseries of Paris, from simple croissants to moist chocolate cakes, piping hot croques-monsieurs and fresh cheeses. I have worked in restaurants for most of my life and thought it might be nice to bring a slice of France to the streets of London. My pop-up, Le Petit Paris, started from a simple idea: I wanted to combine my love of finger food with the classic French cuisine. Snacks should be delicious but also simple and of course small, so you can handle them with your hands.

The dishes you will find in Le Petit Paris *are traditional French recipes with a modern, miniature twist. I hope they inject a hint of Gallic charm into your next celebration, whether it's a lavish party, drinks with friends or a night in.*

Nathalie Benezet

LE PETIT
PARIS
———
Savoury

CROQUE MONSIEUR

Always popular with adults and children – serve for a quick lunch or cut into two triangles and enjoy with drinks. Alternatively cut the sandwiches into four equal squares and pop them on a metal skewer – a great new way to serve this classic dish.

Serves 6 or makes 24 small croques

For the sandwiches

400 ml (13 fl oz/1⅔ cups) whole milk

4 medium egg yolks, beaten

300 g (10½ oz/2½ cups) Gruyère, grated

12 slices white bread, crusts removed

6 slices ham

40 g (1½ oz/3 tablespoons) butter,
    at room temperature

freshly ground black pepper

For the béchamel sauce

15 g (½ oz/1 tablespoon) unsalted butter

15 g (½ oz/1½ tablespoons) plain
    (all-purpose) flour

250 ml (8½ fl oz/1 cup) whole milk

sea salt and freshly ground black pepper

pinch of grated nutmeg

For the sandwich filling, whisk the milk and beaten egg yolks in a medium bowl, season with black pepper, whisk again and stir in the Gruyère. Set aside for at least 30 minutes.

Preheat the oven to 170°C (340°F/gas mark 3½). Line 2 baking trays with baking parchment.

To make the béchamel sauce, melt the butter in a small saucepan over a medium heat. Add the flour and stir over a low heat for 2 minutes. Remove from the heat and gradually add the milk, whisking constantly until the mixture is slightly thick and smooth. Season with salt and pepper and stir in the nutmeg. Return the pan to a gentle heat and whisk continually for 2 minutes or until the sauce has thickened. Be careful not to burn it. Remove from the heat.

Place half the bread slices on to the prepared baking trays. Top each piece of bread with a slice of ham and some of the béchamel sauce. Spread the remaining 6 slices of bread with the butter. Top each sandwich with a piece of buttered bread, butter side uppermost. Drain the Gruyère cheese and sprinkle it on top of the bread.

Bake for 10 minutes or until they are golden brown. Cut each sandwich into 4 equal squares to serve.

EGG MAYONNAISE

Home-made mayo spiced with a dash or two of Worcestershire and Tabasco sauces turns these simple hard-boiled eggs into a real treat. Gem lettuce leaves make perfect little nests for serving.

Makes 16

4 medium or large eggs

1 egg yolk

1 teaspoon Dijon mustard

100 ml (3½ fl oz/scant ½ cup)
   groundnut (peanut) oil

½ teaspoon white wine vinegar

1 teaspoon Worcestershire sauce

3 drops Tabasco sauce (optional)

sea salt and freshly ground black pepper

16 little gem (bibb) lettuce leaves

2 teaspoons snipped chives

Bring a large saucepan of salted water to the boil and cook the eggs – 9 minutes for medium-sized eggs; 10 minutes for large ones. Drain the eggs and rinse under cold running water until cool. Remove the shells.

To make the mayonnaise, whisk the egg yolk in a small bowl then stir in the mustard. Gradually add the oil, drop by drop, whisking until the mixture begins to thicken and become pale in colour. Continue drizzling in the oil until you have the consistency you like. Add a few drops of white wine vinegar and the Worcestershire sauce. For an extra kick, add some Tabasco. Season and mix well.

Cut the shelled eggs into quarters. Arrange the lettuce leaves on a serving plate and place a quarter of egg into each one. Pop a spoonful of mayonnaise on top or serve alongside. Sprinkle over some snipped chives to garnish.

MOULES MARINIÈRES

Serve these fragrant steamed mussels with French fries (page 45) for an authentic Parisian taste. Or for an even simpler, yet equally delicious meal, serve with hunks of crusty baguette to soak up all the flavoursome juices.

Serves 4

50 g (2 oz/¼ cup) butter

4 shallots, chopped

1 celery stalk, chopped

2 garlic cloves, crushed

½ bunch of flat-leaf parsley, finely chopped

400 ml (13 fl oz/1⅔ cups) dry white wine

2 kg (4 lb 6 oz) live mussels, scrubbed and
    beards removed (discard any that stay open
    when sharply tapped)

150 ml (5 fl oz/⅔ cup) double (heavy) cream

sea salt and freshly ground black pepper

Melt the butter in a large saucepan and cook the shallots, celery, garlic and half the parsley over a medium heat, stirring occasionally, until the shallots are softened but not brown. Add the wine to the pan and bring to the boil for 2 minutes.

Tip in the mussels, cover the pan tightly and simmer over a low heat for 2–3 minutes, shaking the pan occasionally.

Use a slotted spoon to remove the cooked mussels and transfer them to a warm dish. Discard any mussels that do not open.

Strain the cooking liquid through a fine sieve into a clean saucepan, leaving behind any grit or sand. Bring to the boil for 2 minutes. Remove from the heat, add the cream, then reheat gently without boiling. Season well.

Serve the mussels in individual bowls with the sauce poured over. Sprinkle with the remaining parsley and eat whilst still hot.

Bêtes du Sud s
on premier long métr
odyssée fantastique, fab
cinéaste invite à une expé
isuel garanti avec un univers
émotionnel d'une intensité rare
nt, les habitants qui vivent dans la
vités à évacuer. Hushpuppy, 6 ans, veut rester
alade tout en rêvant de retrouver sa mère. On a peur, on rit,
re devant la rage la détermination de l'étonnante petite
hané tandis que la tempête gronde et que surgissent des
uvages. Un hymne poignant aux oubliés de Katrina. B.T.
nt, il lui
out en la remette
est exactement la rel
cherchait. Dwight Henry
oulanger. On n'aurait donc au
acteur professionnel pour tenir
cap en plateau ! L'apocalypse que
vous voyez à l'écran, on l'a vécue
tous les jours dans le bayou. »
Le plan de tournage a changé
vingt fois, le village créé avec du
matériel de récupération prenait
nouvelle pépite de l'animation française

PRUNES IN CRISPY BACON

This delicious combination provides a mouthful of contrasts – crispy savoury bacon and soft, melting sweet prunes – great served hot or cold. Substitute the prunes with dried apricots for an equally tasty alternative.

Makes 8

vegetable oil, for greasing

4 streaky bacon rashers (strips)

8 soft dried pitted prunes

Preheat the oven to 200°C (400°F/gas mark 6). Brush a baking tray with the oil.

Cut each bacon rasher in half lengthways. Lay a strip of bacon on a chopping board, place a dried prune at the top edge and roll, wrapping it tightly around the prune. Pierce a cocktail stick through the centre of the wrapped prune to secure. Repeat with the remaining bacon and prunes.

Place the prunes on a the prepared baking tray and bake them for 10–15 minutes, turning over half way through cooking, until the bacon is slightly crispy on both sides.

CAMEMBERT FONDUE

Probably the easiest (and definitely one of the tastiest) cheese fondues ever!
Use the wooden box that the Camembert comes in as a cooking and serving
container. Simply eat with chunks of fruit or crusty bread threaded
onto skewers, to dip into the hot, melted cheese.

Serves 4–6

1 x 250 g (9 oz) Camembert (in a wooden
    box), at room temperature

sea salt and freshly ground black pepper

2 sprigs thyme

1 sprig rosemary

1 tablespoon olive oil

2 tablespoons clear honey

baguette and fresh fruit, cut into bite-sized
    chunks, to serve

Preheat the oven to 200°C (400°F/gas mark 6). Line a baking tray with greaseproof paper.

Remove the Camembert from its box and unwrap. Return the Camembert to its box, and place the box on the lined baking tray.

Carefully, using a sharp knife, slice the rind at the top about 4–5 times. This will allow the flavours to infuse inside the cheese.

Sprinkle sea salt and black pepper over the cheese, stick the thyme and rosemary sprigs into the rind and drizzle with the olive oil and honey. Bake for 20 minutes until the cheese is melted inside.

Leave to cool slightly before serving. Dip slices of crusty baguette or pieces of fruit into the soft cheese and enjoy.

ONION SOUP

Slowly caramelised onions, white wine and stock form the basis of this richly comforting soup. For the finishing touch, sprinkle over a generous handful of crisp, cheesy croutons and serve piping hot.

Serves 4 as a starter or 12 as a mini appetiser

250 ml (8½ fl oz/1 cup) dry white wine

50 g (2 oz/¼ cup) butter

750 g (1 lb 10 oz/5 cups) onions, finely sliced

sea salt and freshly ground black pepper

1 garlic clove, finely sliced

40g (1½ oz/⅓ cup) plain (all-purpose) flour

1.75 litres (3 pints/7½ cups) beef or
　　chicken stock

½ teaspoon sugar (optional)

6 x 2 cm (¾ in) slices stale baguette

250 g (9 oz/2 cups) Gruyère, finely grated

flat-leaf parsley, finely chopped, for garnish

Pour the wine into a small pan over a high heat. Bring to the boil and allow to bubble for 30 seconds to remove the alcohol.

Melt the butter in a heavy-based saucepan over a low heat. Add the onions, season and cook very gently for 25 minutes, or until the onions are golden brown and beginning to caramelise.

Add the garlic and flour to the pan and stir continuously for 2 minutes. Gradually add the stock and wine, stirring continuously, and bring to the boil. Cover the pan and simmer for 25 minutes. Taste and adjust the seasoning and add the sugar if required.

Preheat the grill to high. Cut the baguette slices in half and spread on a baking tray. Sprinkle with two thirds of the grated Gruyère and place under the grill for 3–4 minutes to melt and slightly brown the cheese. Cut the slices of baguette into bite-sized pieces.

Ladle the soup into 4 heatproof bowls, and sprinkle over the remaining cheese. Add a few croutons to each dish and place under the grill until the cheese melts and turns a light golden-brown. Sprinkle with parsley and serve immediately.

BEEF TARTARE

For the very best results, rather than buying ready-minced beef for these tasty little mouthfuls, I recommend you use top quality beef, such as rump or sirloin. Then mince or finely chop it yourself, or get your butcher to do it for you once you've chosen the steak.

Makes 12

4 egg yolks

½ teaspoon sunflower oil

1 teaspoon Worcestershire sauce

½ teaspoon tomato ketchup

8 drops Tabasco sauce

400 g (14 oz) rump (round) or sirloin
   steak, minced (ground) or very
   finely chopped

2 teaspoons capers, drained and finely
   chopped

2 gherkins, drained and finely chopped

1 shallot, finely chopped

½ onion, finely chopped

¼ bunch of flat leaf parsley, finely chopped,
   plus extra to garnish

sea salt and freshly ground black pepper

½ baguette

Whisk 2 of the egg yolks in a large bowl. Add the oil, Worcestershire sauce, ketchup and the Tabasco and whisk well to combine.

Add the chopped steak to the dressing along with the capers, gherkins, shallots, onion and parsley. Mix thoroughly to combine and season well.

Preheat the grill to high. Slice the baguette into 12 equal pieces and toast under the grill, on both sides, until golden. Place on a serving plate.

Beat the remaining egg yolks together in a small bowl.

Using a 4 cm (1½ in) round pastry cutter, shape the tartare mixture into 12 equal rounds. Top each slice of toast with a round of beef, make a little indentation in each round and, using a teaspoon, pour in a little of the beaten egg yolk. Garnish with parsley, to serve.

NIÇOISE SALAD

Appetising little parcels of this popular salad, made with cherry tomatoes and quail's eggs, look great served on large platters for guests to help themselves. Pop a basket of thinly sliced baguette on the table too, to go with the salad.

Makes 20

125 g (4 oz/1 cup) fine green beans

10 quail's eggs

20 little gem (bibb) lettuce leaves

10 cherry tomatoes, halved

10 pitted black olives, halved

250 g (9 oz) can best quality tuna in olive oil, drained

For the Vinaigrette

1 garlic clove, crushed

1 teaspoon Dijon mustard

2 tablespoons white wine vinegar

1 teaspoon lemon juice

125 ml (½ cup) olive oil

sea salt and freshly ground pepper

Bring a medium pan of salted water to the boil and add the beans. Simmer for 3–4 minutes or until just cooked. Drain and refresh under cold running water.

Place a medium pan of cold water on the hob and heat over a medium heat. Once the water starts to gently simmer add the quail's eggs. Bring to the boil and cook for 1–2 minutes. Drain and cool under cold running water. Remove the eggs shells and cut them in half.

To make the vinaigrette, whisk together the garlic, mustard, vinegar and lemon juice. Add the oil carefully, in a steady stream, whisking until smooth. Season to taste.

Arrange the lettuce leaves on serving plates and place half an egg, half a tomato and half an olive in each leaf. Top with a few green beans and a chunk of tuna. Serve with the vinaigrette.

FOIE GRAS BURGERS

Home-made burgers are always popular and these sophisticated mini morsels are really special. If you can't get a hold of foie gras, use a good quality minced beef instead.

Makes 20

For the buns

300 g (10½ oz/2½ cups) strong (hard wheat) white flour, sifted plus extra for dusting

1 teaspoon easy-blend dried yeast

1 teaspoon salt

3 teaspoons olive oil, plus extra for oiling

170 ml (6 fl oz/¾ cup) warm water

2 teaspoons sesame seeds (optional)

For the burgers

200 g (7 oz) foie gras, finely cubed

600 g (1 lb 5 oz) beef, finely chopped

sea salt and freshly ground black pepper

sunflower oil, for frying

To serve

50 g (2 oz) unsalted butter, at room temperature

4 small tomatoes, sliced

12 little gem (bib) lettuce leaves

French fries (page 45)

To make the buns, put the flour, yeast and salt in a food processor fitted with a dough hook. Make a well in the centre, add the oil and warm water and mix on a low speed to combine.

Remove from the bowl and knead on a floured surface for 15 minutes or until the dough is smooth and elastic. Place in an oiled bowl, cover with a clean tea towel and leave in a warm place for 45 minutes or until the dough has doubled in size.

Preheat the oven to 240°C (475°F/gas mark 9). Line 2 baking trays with baking parchment.

Divide the dough into 20 equal pieces, roll each into a ball and place on the trays. Press lightly to flatten slightly and sprinkle with a little salt and a few sesame seeds, if using. Leave in a warm place for 30 minutes, or until the buns have doubled in size, then bake for 15–20 minutes or until golden. Transfer to a wire rack to cool.

Meanwhile, place the foie gras and beef in a large bowl, season and mix well to combine. Shape the mixture into 20 equal patties.

Heat the oil in a large non-stick frying pan over a medium–high heat and fry the patties in batches, for 2–3 minutes on each side, or until cooked medium rare.

To serve, halve each bun and spread with a little butter. Place a patty on the bottom half of each bun, top with a slice of tomato, some lettuce and the remaining half of the bun top. Secure with a cocktail stick and serve with French fries on the side.

CELERIAC REMOULADE

This remoulade is a classic French dish and makes perfect use of an under-used vegetable. Choose from capers, parsley or gherkins (or any combination of all three), to add flavour and a pretty hint of green. The celeriac will discolour and brown as soon as it is peeled and sliced, so either use it straight away or soak in water with lemon juice added, for up to 1 hour before using.

Makes 15–20 or serves 4 as a side dish

2 celeriac

juice of 1 lemon

For the remoulade sauce

2 egg yolks

1 teaspoon white wine vinegar

1 teaspoon Dijon mustard

120 ml (4 fl oz/½ cup) olive oil

sea salt and freshly ground black pepper

To serve

2 teaspoon capers, drained (optional)

2 teaspoons finely chopped flat-leaf parsley (optional)

5 gherkins, drained and finely chopped (optional)

4 teaspoons peanuts, finely chopped

Use a sharp knife to carefully peel the celeriac and remove the knobbly outer surface. Put 1 litre (34 fl oz/ 4 cups) cold water and half the lemon juice in a large bowl. Cut the celeriac into thin julienne strips and put them immediately into the lemon water to prevent discoloration. Soak for up to 1 hour.

Bring a large saucepan of water to the boil and add the remaining lemon juice. Drain the celeriac and add to the boiling water. After 1 minute, drain and cool under cold running water. Pat dry with paper towels.

To make the remoulade, whisk the egg yolks, vinegar and mustard together in a bowl. Add the oil, drop by drop from the tip of a teaspoon, whisking constantly until the mixture begins to thicken, then add the remaining oil in a very thin stream. Season and, if necessary, thin with a little warm water.

Fold the celeriac strips into the remoulade and chill for 2–4 hours. Stir in the finely chopped capers, parsley and gherkins, if using, and sprinkle with the chopped peanuts before serving.

CHEESE GOUGÈRES

These bite-sized cheesy choux pastry puffs are best served warm from the oven – they are so delicious you will probably find they've all have disappeared before they've had a chance to cool down!

Makes 30

120 ml (4 fl oz/½ cup) milk

100 g (3½ oz/scant ½ cup) butter, cubed

1 teaspoon salt

pinch of sugar

freshly ground black pepper

150 g (5 oz/1¼ oz) plain (all-purpose) flour

5 eggs, beaten

125 g (4 oz/1 cup) Gruyère or Comté, grated

50 g (2 oz/1/2 cup) parmesan, grated

Preheat the oven to 190°C (375°F/gas mark 5) and line 2 baking trays with baking paper.

Place the milk and 120 ml (4 fl oz/½ cup) water in a large heavy-based saucepan. Add the butter, salt, sugar and pepper and heat gently over a moderate heat. As soon as the water boils and all the butter has melted, remove from the heat.

Add all the flour at once, and beat hard with a wooden spoon until you have a smooth dough that comes away from the sides of the pan without sticking. Return the pan to the hob and continue to beat the dough over a low heat for a couple of minutes more. It will begin to thicken and dry.

Transfer the dough into a food processor or a mixing bowl (if making by hand), and allow to cool for 5 minutes. Gradually add the eggs to the dough, a quarter at a time. Beat well after each addition. Continue beating until all the eggs have been incorporated and the dough is completely smooth. Add the grated Gruyère or Comté and 2 tablespoons of the parmesan and stir well, to combine.

Spoon the dough into a piping bag fitted with a 1 cm (½ in) plain nozzle. Pipe 30 x 2 cm (¾ in) rounds of dough onto the trays leaving 2 cm (¾ in) gaps between. Sprinkle with the remaining parmesan and bake for 20 minutes or until golden and crisp. After 15 minutes of cooking, gently open the oven door for the last 5 minutes. This helps to create more steam in the oven and the puffs rise better.

Transfer to a wire cooling rack for 5 minutes and then serve. These are best eaten on the day you make them.

OYSTERS

Oysters that have just been opened or shucked have the very best flavour. Use a special shucking (oyster-opening) knife, if possible, to prepare your oysters otherwise use a short knife with a strong, sharp blade. If you'd prefer, ask your fishmonger to shuck them for you, but you'll need to eat the oysters on the day you buy them.

Makes 24

For the shallot vinegar

4 shallots, finely chopped

100 ml (3½ fl oz/scant ½ cup)
    red wine vinegar

24 live oysters in their shells, scrubbed
    (discard any that stay open when
    sharply tapped)

1 lemon, cut into wedges

Mix the shallots and vinegar together in a bowl and set aside to infuse for 1 hour.

Hold an oyster firmly with a tea towel over a bowl (to catch any liquid). Insert the point of an oyster sharp knife into the hinged edge and twist to open. Carefully run the edge of the knife along the inside of the top shell to cut the muscle away. Lift off the top shell and cut underneath the oyster to release it. Rinse the oysters to remove any bits of shell and put to one side. Wash and dry the shells then pop the oysters back in.

Serve the oysters, shallot vinegar and lemon wedges separately so guests can spoon the mixture and squeeze the lemon onto the oysters themselves.

PROVENÇAL TARTLETS

Equally delicious served hot or cold, these colourful mini tarts are packed full of the flavours of summer. They can be made well in advance and frozen. Simply defrost them at room temperature for 2–3 hours.

Makes 36

For the shortcrust pastry

300 g (10½ oz/21½ cups) plain

   (all-purpose) flour, plus extra for dusting

175 g (6 oz/scant ¾ cup) chilled unsalted

   butter, cubed

pinch of salt

1 egg yolk

For the filling

5 tomatoes

1 teaspoons olive oil, plus extra for brushing

½ of a large white onion, finely chopped

1 teaspoon tomato purée (paste)

1 garlic clove, finely chopped

½ teaspoon oregano, roughly chopped,

   plus a few whole leaves to garnish

½ red pepper, halved and deseeded

½ yellow pepper, halved and deseeded

18 tinned anchovies, drained and halved

18 pitted black olives, halved

To make the pastry, place all the ingredients except the egg, in a food processor and pulse until the mixture resembles breadcrumbs. Add the egg yolk and 2 tablespoons of cold water and pulse again until the dough starts to come together. Transfer the dough to a floured surface and knead. Shape into a ball, wrap in plastic wrap and refrigerate for 1 hour.

For the filling, heat the oil in a frying pan, add the onion, cover and cook over low heat for 20 minutes or the onion has softened but not browned. Meanwhile, place the tomatoes in a bowl and cover with boiling water. Leave for 1 minute, remove and set aside to cool then peel and chop. Add the tomatoes with the tomato purée, garlic and oregano to the frying pan and simmer for 20 minutes, stirring occasionally. Once the tomatoes are soft and the mixture has become a paste, set aside to cool.

Roll out the pastry on a floured surface to a thickness of 5 mm (½ in). Using a small round pastry cutter, cut out enough discs to fill a 24-hole and a 12-hole mini tart tin. Prick the base of the cases with a fork, cover with plastic wrap and chill for 30 minutes.

Preheat the oven to 200°C (400°F/gas mark 6) and preheat the grill to high. Place the halved peppers skin-side-up, under the hot grill until the skin blackens. Cool, peel and cut into thin strips. Cut out small squares of baking paper and line the mini pastry cases. Fill each case with a few baking beans. Bake the cases for 5 minutes, then remove the paper and beans and bake until the pastry is just cooked but still very pale. Reduce the oven temperature to 180°C (350°F/gas mark 4).

Spread a little tomato paste in each tart case then scatter with pepper strips. Arrange the anchovies and olives on the top, brush with olive oil and bake for 20 minutes. Scatter with oregano leaves to serve.

37

PARISIAN SANDWICH

Aged Gruyère has a stronger flavour than the more creamy, nutty, younger variety, and give these sandwiches a wonderfully distinctive taste. For an authentic French rustic look, secure each sandwich with string and serve with cornichons — tiny pickled gherkins.

Makes 12

1 baguette

butter at room temperature, for spreading

6 thin slices jambon de Paris ham,
    or a similar type of white ham

6 thin slices aged Gruyère

cornichons, to serve

Slice the baguette in half lengthwise, leaving the long edge joined together so you can open it like a book.

Spread butter along both halves of the inside, fold the slices of ham and place along one side of the baguette. Place the cheese on top and sandwich the baguette together.

Cut into 12 equal pieces and tie each piece with string.

Serve with cornichons alongside.

MACARONI CHEESE

*Little dishes of this all-time favourite cheesy pasta dish are lovely
to serve as a starter with crusty bread or as a main course for children
with some steamed green beans or broccoli.*

Serves 6 as a starter

250 g (9 oz/1¾ cups) macaroni

350 g (12 oz/1⅓ cups) crème fraîche

150 ml (5 fl oz/⅔ cup) double
   (thick) cream

150 g (5 oz/1¼ cup) Comté, grated

sea salt and freshly ground black pepper

pinch of grated nutmeg

1 garlic clove, halved

100 g (3½ oz/generous ¾ cup)
   Gruyère, grated

Preheat the oven to 190°C (375°F/gas mark 5).

Cook the macaroni in a large pan of boiling salted water, according to the packet instructions, until al dente. Drain and rinse under cold running water.

Place the crème fraîche and double cream in a large saucepan over a medium heat until it starts to boil. Take off the heat when it starts to bubble and stir in the Comté, until melted. Season to taste and stir in the nutmeg.

Rub the halved garlic clove around the inside of 6 ramekins. Tip the cooked pasta in to the cheese sauce and mix well.

Place the ramekins on a baking tray and spoon the mixture evenly between the ramekins, sprinkle with the Gruyère and bake, uncovered, for 15 minutes.

Turn on the grill to high. Place the ramekins under the hot grill for a few minutes before serving for a slightly caramelised crispy topping.

PUFF PASTRY TWISTS

Crisp golden pastry with flakes of nutty Gruyère cheese – the perfect accompaniment to a glass of chilled white on a hot day or a robust red on a chilly autumn evening. In fact these go with pretty much any drink for a delicious pre-dinner nibble.

Serves 4

320 g pack ready rolled puff pastry

flour, for dusting

1 large egg, beaten

250 g (9 oz/2 cups) Gruyère, grated

Preheat the oven to 220°C (430°F/gas mark 7). Line two baking sheets with baking paper.

Carefully unfold the pastry on a lightly floured surface and cut it into 2 equal-sized rectangles. Brush half the egg over one of the rectangles and sprinkle the cheese evenly over, right to the edges of the pastry. Brush the remaining egg over the second rectangle and place it, egg side down, on top of the cheese-covered pastry. Lightly roll the 2 sheets together with a rolling pin to seal.

With a sharp knife cut the cheese and pastry sandwich into strips about 1 cm (½ in) wide. One at a time, hold the ends of each strip and twist in opposite directions to form a spiral. Transfer to the prepared baking sheets and bake for about 10 minutes or until a light golden brown. Remove from the oven and cool on the baking sheets until cool enough to handle. Serve either warm or at room temperature.

STEAK AU POIVRE

I like to serve these melt-in-the-mouth cubes of steak in tiny pans or dessertspoons. You could also serve the sauce in a bowl with the pieces of steak on skewers for guests to dip in.

Makes 12 miniature steaks

2 x 200 g (7 oz) fillet steaks (beef tenderloin)

2 teaspoons olive oil

4 teaspoons black peppercorns, crushed

20 g (1½ oz/3 tablespoons) butter

3 teaspoons cognac

4 tablespoons white wine

100 ml (3½ fl oz/½ cup) double (thick) cream

sea salt and freshly ground black pepper

Rub the steaks on both sides with the oil and press the crushed peppercorns into the meat. Melt the butter in a large frying pan and cook the steaks for 2–4 minutes on each side, depending on how you like your steak.

Add the cognac and light it to flambé with a gas flame or a match. Transfer the steaks to a hot plate and wrap in foil to keep warm.

Add the wine to the pan and boil for 1 minute, stirring to deglaze the pan. Add the cream and stir for 1–2 minutes. Season with more fresh black pepper from the pepper mill.

Cut each steak into 6 bite-size pieces and serve with a spoonful of sauce.

FRENCH FRIES

You can't beat home-made fries and for the very best, 'crunchy-on-the outside and fluffy-in-the-middle' combination, the right type of potato makes a big difference. So for best results, choose a waxy potato such as Maris Peer, Cara or Marfona.

500 g (1 lb 2 oz) potatoes, per person

3 litres (5 pints / 12 cup) groundnut (peanut) oil, for deep frying

salt

Advance preparation is the key to making perfect French fries. Peel and slice the potatoes into long sticks about 5 mm (¼ in) thick. Rinse the sticks under cold running water and leave in a large bowl of cold water so they don't turn brown.

Bring a large saucepan of unsalted water to the boil. Add the potato sticks and boil for 2 minutes, then drain and spread out on paper towels. Thoroughly pat the sticks dry, using plenty of paper towels – repeat twice or three times until they are very dry. They will only become crispy when very dry.

Heat the oil in a large pan over a medium-high heat or in a deep fat fryer to 140°C (275°F). Make sure that you have at least 7.5 cm (3 inches) between the top of the oil and the top of the pan. Carefully lower the potato sticks into the fat and fry for 10 minutes stirring occasionally, until the potatoes are soft and limp and begin to turn a light golden colour. Do this in batches if necessary. Remove with a slotted spoon, drain on paper towels and leave to rest for at least 10 minutes. Fries can be made to this point up to 2 hours in advance of serving.

For the second frying increase the heat of the oil to 160°C (325°F) and transfer the blanched potatoes to the hot oil for 2–3 minutes. Stir frequently until the fries are puffed and golden brown. Remove with a slotted spoon and drain on more paper towels. Season immediately with salt and serve hot.

Cooked fries can be kept hot and crisp for up to 10 minutes on a wire rack on a baking tray in a 170°C (340°F/gas mark 3½) oven.

CRUSTLESS QUICHETTES

Imagine the light and airy yet rich and creamy filling of a quiche in a single mouthful, well that's exactly what these are! If you prefer a vegetarian option, substitute the bacon for finely chopped mushrooms and peppers.

Makes 18

butter, for greasing

300 g (10½ oz) streaky bacon or smoked
   ham, diced

3 eggs

3 egg yolks

250 ml (8½ fl oz/1 cup) double
   (thick) cream

sea salt and freshly ground black pepper

150 g (5 oz/1¼ cups) Gruyère, grated

Preheat the oven to 180°C (350°F/gas mark 4). Butter an 18-hole mini muffin or tartlet tin.

Fry the bacon or smoked ham in a heavy-based frying pan for 3–4 minutes over a medium heat until crispy and golden. Drain on paper towels and leave to cool.

Beat the eggs and egg yolks in a bowl. Add the cream and mix together, then season with salt and pepper. Scatter the bacon in the greased tart tin and pour over the egg mixture. Sprinkle some grated Gruyère on top of each quiche and bake for 10–12 minutes until golden.

PARISIAN ASPARAGUS

Fresh, tender asparagus is the star of the show here – served cold with a smooth, creamy sauce for dipping, it makes a seasonal savoury treat at the beginning of summer.

Serves 4

salt

24 asparagus, woody ends trimmed

2 medium egg yolks

2 teaspoons lemon juice

sea salt and freshly ground black pepper

90 g (3¼ oz) unslated butter, cut into cubes

Bring a saucepan of salted water to the boil, add the asparagus and simmer for 4 minutes, or until just tender. Drain, then cool under cold running water.

To make the sauce, whisk the egg yolks and lemon juice in a saucepan over a very low heat. Keep whisking and add the butter piece by piece, until the sauce thickens. Do not over heat the sauce otherwise the eggs will scramble.

Once the sauce has thickened and all the butter has been added, turn the heat off, and set aside to cool.

Serve the asparagus spears with the cooled sauce on the side.

GRATIN DAUPHINOIS

These miniature gratins are an exciting and quite luxurious way of serving potatoes. Make sure the layers are as flat as possible so there are no gaps that will hold too much cream.

Makes 8

1.5 kg (3 lb 5 oz) floury potatoes
    e.g. Estima, King Edward or Maris Piper

3 garlic cloves

30 g (1 oz/2 tablespoons) butter

2 pinches of grated nutmeg

salt and freshly ground black pepper

400 ml (13 fl oz/1⅔ cups) double
    (thick) cream

3 teaspoons milk

100 g (3½ oz/generous ¾ cup)
Gruyère, grated

Preheat the oven to 180°C (350°F/gas mark 4).

Peel the potatoes and cut into 5 mm (¼ in) slices (use a mandolin if you have one). Dry them with kitchen towel.

Cut one of the garlic cloves in half and finely chop the remainder. Rub the inside of 8 ramekins with the cut garlic then grease with the butter. Place the ramekins on a baking tray. Arrange the potato slices in layers in the dishes, sprinkling the crushed garlic, nutmeg and seasoning between the layers. Mix the cream and milk together in a jug, then divide it equally among the dishes. Sprinkle with the Gruyère and dot the remaining butter on top.

Bake for 35 minutes or until the potatoes are completely cooked and the liquid has absorbed.

COARSE PORK PÂTÉ

Serve this pâté, also known as rillettes, on crackers or toast with a few tangy cornichons for a traditional starter or snack. The pâté will keep for one week, in an airtight container, in the fridge.

Makes 40 small toasts

425 g (15 oz) belly pork

125 g (4 oz/½ cup) lard (shortening) or butter

¾ teaspoon sea salt

½ teaspoon freshly ground black pepper

1 bay leaf

½ sprig rosemary

1 sprig thyme

crackers or toast and cornichons, to serve

Cut the pork into large pieces and place in a large saucepan with the lard or butter. Pour in 500 ml (17 fl oz/generous 2 cups) cold water to cover the meat. Add the seasoning and herbs and bring to the boil, then lower the heat and continue to cook over a gentle heat for 3 hours. Check that all the water has been absorbed – keep cooking until it has – then remove from the heat and set aside to cool.

Once cool, remove the herbs. Shred the meat using a couple of forks, or pulse very briefly in a food processor until you have a rough paste – you don't want the texture to be too smooth.

Taste and adjust the seasoning, then pack the meat into 4 ramekins. Cover with plastic wrap and chill in the fridge for a minimum of 24 hours. The fat will harden when chilled so you will need to break up the pâté with a fork before serving. Serve with crackers or mini toasts and cornichons.

SCRAMBLED EGGS WITH TRUFFLES

To make the most of the delicious flavour of the truffles, you need to be a bit organised and put the eggs and truffles in the fridge together overnight, to allow the flavours to permeate the eggs. Serve the eggs in the eggshells, but if you have trouble keeping the shells intact, simply use eggcups or ramekins instead.

Serves 8

8 large eggs (preferably organic)

80 g (3 oz/1 cup) fresh black truffle, plus 20g (¾ oz/¼ cup), shaved, to serve

1 garlic clove, halved

50 g (2 oz/¼ cup) butter

sea salt and freshly black ground pepper

The day before cooking, put the eggs and truffle together in an airtight container in the fridge.

Carefully remove the tops of the eggshells and pour the eggs into a bowl. Wash out the eggshells, pat them dry with paper towels, then place into eggcups for serving.

Beat the eggs together. Squash and smash the truffle with a fork (don't cut with a knife – using a fork will give more texture). Add the truffle to the beaten eggs.

Rub the cut edges of the garlic clove around the inside of a small saucepan. Melt the butter in the pan, add the egg mixture and season with salt and freshly ground black pepper. Stir frequently with a small whisk over a low heat for 3 minutes or until the eggs are just beginning to set. Don't overcook the eggs – they should remain slightly runny. Taste and adjust the seasoning if necessary.

Spoon the scrambled eggs into the prepared eggshells and sprinkle with shavings of truffle. Serve immediately.

ESCARGOTS WITH GARLIC BUTTER

You can buy canned snails (escargots) complete with empty shells for serving them in. Eat with chunks of baguette to mop up the garlicky butter.

Makes 24

200 g can snails, well drained

250 ml (8½ fl oz/1 cup) white wine

250 ml (8½ fl oz/1 cup) chicken stock

3 sprigs tarragon

2 garlic cloves, crushed

2 teaspoons finely chopped basil leaves

2 teaspoons finely chopped parsley

2 teaspoons finely chopped tarragon leaves

150 g (5 oz/scant ⅔ cup) butter,
    at room temperature

250 g (9 oz/¾ cup) rock salt

baguette, to serve

Rinse the snails in several changes of fresh water until all the grit has been removed. Put the wine, stock, tarragon sprigs and 120 ml (4 fl oz/½ cup) water in a small saucepan and boil for 2 minutes. Add the snails and simmer for 7 minutes.

Remove from the heat and leave to cool in the pan. When cool, drain and place a snail in each shell.

Preheat the oven to 200°C (400°F/gas mark 6). Mix the garlic, basil, parsley and tarragon into the butter and season well. Put a little garlic butter into each shell and arrange them on a snail plate or baking tray covered with a layer of rock salt. Bake for 7–8 minutes or until the butter melts and the snails are heated through. Serve immediately with crusty bread.

HERBY LAMB CUTLETS

The cutlets used here are usually sold as a rack of lamb.
Either buy an eight-rib rack and cut it into individual 2 cm (1 inch) chops
yourself, or ask your butcher to cut it for you.

Serves 4

8 lamb rib cutlets

4 teaspoons olive oil

1 teaspoon chopped rosemary leaves

1 teaspoon chopped thyme leaves

sea salt and freshly ground black pepper

1 lemon cut into wedges, to serve

Heat a griddle pan over a medium-high heat. Mix the oil and herbs in a bowl, then rub all over the meat.

Arrange the cutlets in the pan at a 45° angle to the ridges. Cook for 1 minute then move the cutlets around on the ridges to form the standard criss-cross markings on the underside. Cook for a further 1 minute. Turn the cutlets over and repeat on the other side.

The cutlets will cook quickly and can be eaten from medium-rare to well done. Cook your cutlets for 1–3 minutes for medium rare and 3–5 minutes for well done.

When cooked to your liking remove from the heat and rest in a warm place for at least 5 minutes. This allows all the juices to settle back into the meat.

Serve the cutlets with lemon wedges on the side.

PISSALADIÈRE TARTLETS

Based on an onion tart recipe, especially popular in southern France, these savoury bites may be no more than a mouthful, but what they lack in size they certainly make up for in flavour!

Makes approximately 36

For the shortcrust pastry

300 g (10½ oz/2½ cups) plain

    (all-purpose) flour, plus extra for dusting

175 g (6 oz/¾ cup) chilled unsalted

    butter, cubed

pinch of salt

1 egg yolk

vegetable oil, for greasing

For the filling

15 g (½ oz/ 1 tbsp) butter

1 teaspoon olive oil, plus extra for brushing

375 g (13 oz/1½ cups) onions,

    thinly sliced

½ teaspoon thyme leaves, plus extra

    for garnishing

salt and freshly ground black pepper

4 anchovies, halved lengthways

6 pitted olives

To make the pastry, place the flour, butter and salt in a food processor and pulse until the mixture resembles breadcrumbs. Add the egg yolk and 2 tablespoons cold water and pulse again until the dough just starts to come together. Transfer to a floured surface and knead to bring together. Shape the pastry into a disc, wrap in plastic wrap and refrigerate for 1 hour.

Meanwhile, melt the butter and olive oil in a large saucepan. Add the onions and thyme, cover and cook over a low heat for 45 minutes, stirring occasionally, until the onions are softened but not browned. Season and leave to cool.

Preheat the oven to 200°C (400°F). Brush 3 baking trays with the vegetable oil, to grease.

Roll out the pastry on a floured surface to a 15 x 24 cm (6 x 9½ in) rectangle. Cut the pastry into 36 rectangles, approximately 2.5 x 4 cm (1 x 1½ in), and place 12 on each baking tray. Brush each piece with a little olive oil, then spread some onions on top. Arrange a little strip of anchovy and half an olive on each one. Cook for 15 minutes or until the dough is cooked and lightly browned. Garnish with thyme leaves and serve hot or warm.

LE PETIT PARIS

Sweet

CROISSANTS

Homemade croissants really are worth the effort. Serve with jam and fresh coffee for a traditional French breakfast.

Makes 30

For the croissants

600 g (1 lb 5 oz/1¾ cups) strong (hard wheat) white flour, plus extra for dusting

1 tablespoon sea salt

75 g (2½ oz/⅓ cup) caster (superfine) sugar

2 tablespoons milk powder

40 g (1½ oz/3 tablespoons) butter, at room temperature

15 g (½ oz) fresh yeast

200 ml (7 fl oz/scant 1 cup) warm water

1 tablespoon vegetable oil, for greasing

325 g (11 oz/1⅓ cups) chilled butter

50 g (2 oz/¼ cup) clarified butter, melted, for glazing

For the egg wash

2 eggs

1 egg yolk

pinch of salt

Sift the flour into a large bowl and add the salt, sugar, milk powder and butter. Stir the yeast into 120 ml (4 fl oz/½ cup) of the warm water until dissolved and pour into the bowl. Mix the dough until all the ingredients are combined. Add the remaining water if the dough seems too firm. Knead the dough lightly on a floured surface. Cover the bowl with oiled plastic wrap and leave to rise at warm room temperature for at least 1 hour.

When the dough has doubled in size, transfer to a board and push down on it using your fists (knock back) until it is the original size. Return to the bowl, cover with plastic wrap and refrigerate for 1 hour. Remove and repeat this technique. Wrap the dough and chill in a freezer for 30 minutes.

Roll the dough into a rectangle, approximately the size of a standard baking tray. Work the cold butter with a spoon to soften it. Spread half the butter on the lower two thirds of the rectangle and then fold. Fold the dough again without adding butter and repeat again with the remaining butter. You should end up with 3 layers. Rest the dough for approximately 20 minutes then repeat this rolling and folding process 3 times, leaving at least 20 minutes between each rolling and folding.

Preheat the oven to 220°C (430°F/gas mark 7). Line your baking trays with baking paper, and grease with a little oil. Roll out the dough into a rectangle approximately 2.5 mm thick. Cut triangles approximately 10 cm (4 in) x 8 cm (3 1/4 in) x 8 cm (3¼ in). Roll each triangle from the base and curve them into a croissant shape. Place them on the baking sheet, leaving a 5 cm (2 in) space between them and leave to rise for 1½–2 hours at room temperature. Meanwhile, whisk the ingredients together to make the egg wash. Once the croissants have risen, brush them with the egg wash.

Lower the oven temperature to 190°C (375°F/gas mark 5) and bake for 20 minutes. Whilst still hot from the oven brush the croissants lightly with the melted clarified butter to glaze. Cool on a wire rack. Serve with a dollop of jam and a hot drink.

CLAFOUTIS

Traditionally cherries are used in this dish, but other soft fruits, such as a mixture of raspberries, blueberries and blackcurrants or chopped plums, peaches or nectarines work just as well.

Makes 15–20

1 vanilla pod

170 ml (6 fl oz/¾ cup) double (thick) cream

120 ml (4 fl oz/½ cup) milk

3 eggs

100 g (3½ oz/½ cup) caster (superfine) sugar

80 g (3 oz/½ cup) plain (all-purpose) flour

200 g (7 oz/1 cup) cherries, pitted and halved

icing (confectioner's) sugar, for dusting

Preheat the oven to 180°C (350°F/gas mark 4).

Split the vanilla pod in two lengthways, scrape out the seeds and add the pod and seeds to a small saucepan with the cream. Heat gently for a couple of minutes, then remove from the heat, add the milk and cool. Strain through a fine sieve, into a large bowl, to remove the pod.

Whisk the eggs with the sugar and flour, then stir into the cream mixture. Divide half the cherries equally between 15–20 mini ramekins. Add the remaining fruit to the batter and stir well.

Place the ramekins on baking trays and divide the batter equally between them. Bake for 15–20 minutes or until golden on top. Dust with icing sugar and serve warm or cold.

FINANCIERS

Light almond sponge cakes with a crispy outer and soft centre, dotted with tangy blueberries – perfect with a cup of tea. Traditionally they were made to resemble golden bricks, which is how they originally got their name.

Makes 30

50 g (2 oz/¼ cup) butter plus extra
    for greasing

50 g (2 oz/½ cup) plain (all-purpose) flour
    plus extra for dusting

140 g (4½ oz/1⅓ cups) ground almonds

160 g (5½ oz/1⅓ cups) icing
    (confectioner's) sugar, plus extra for dusting

6 egg whites, at room temperature

50 g (2 oz/⅓ cup) blueberries, washed
    and dried

Butter 30 x 6 cm (2½ in) financier tins, dust lightly with flour and chill in the fridge until needed.

Gently heat the butter in a small pan over a medium heat until it turns a dark golden brown, then immediately remove from the heat.

Mix together all the dry ingredients in a large bowl then stir in the egg whites. Gradually stir in the hot butter until you have a smooth batter. Cover and refrigerate for 2 hours.

Preheat the oven to 180°C (350°F/gas mark 4).

Spoon the batter into the chilled tins until they are three quarters full, then pop a few blueberries into each one. Bake for 10–12 minutes until firm and golden brown.

Remove from the oven and leave to cool in the tins for a few minutes. Transfer to a wire rack and dust with icing sugar to serve.

CHOCOLATE MOUSSE

Use a selection of pretty small glasses to serve this classic French mousse.
It can be made up to a couple of days in advance.

Makes 15–20

200 g (7 oz/1⅓ cups) dark (bittersweet)
   chocolate (minimum 70% cocoa solids),
   broken into pieces

4 teaspoons butter

pinch of salt

1 teaspoon vanilla extract (optional)

4 eggs, separated

2 teaspoons sugar

250 ml (8½ fl oz/1 cup) whipping cream

125 g (4 oz/1 cup) raspberries

Place the chocolate and butter in a large, heatproof bowl over a pan of gently simmering water. Stir until melted. Remove from the heat and add the salt and vanilla essence and mix until smooth. Add the egg yolks, one by one, stirring well after each addition, and set aside.

Place the egg whites in a large bowl and whisk until soft peaks form. Add the sugar and continue beating until stiff, glossy peaks form. Mix a quarter of the beaten whites into the chocolate mixture and fold in the rest gently with a plastic spatula.

Lightly whisk the whipping cream until thickened, then fold gently into the mousse.

Divide the raspberries between the serving glasses and spoon the mousse over the top (it's easier to use a piping bag if the glasses are very small). Cover with plastic wrap and chill for at least 3 hours before serving.

ICE CREAM PROFITEROLES

*Vanilla and chocolate ice creams work well together as fillings here,
but experiment and use whichever flavours are your favourites.*

Makes 20

For the choux pastry

120 ml (4 fl oz/½ cup) milk

100 g (3½ oz/scant ½ cup) butter, cubed

1 teaspoon salt

1 teaspoon sugar

140 g (4½ oz/1¼ cups) plain
 (all-purpose) flour

5 eggs, beaten

For the sauce

150 g (5 oz/1 cup) dark (bittersweet)
 chocolate (minimum 70% cocoa solids),
 finely chopped

20 g (¾ oz/3 tablespoons) butter

20 g (¾ oz/2 tablespoons) sugar

120 ml (4 fl oz/½ cup) double (thick) cream

For the filling

1 litre (34 fl oz/4 cups) vanilla or chocolate
 ice cream

Preheat the oven to 190°C (375°F/gas mark 5) and line 2 baking trays with baking paper.

Place the milk and 120 ml (4 fl oz/½ cup) water in a large heavy-based saucepan. Add the butter, salt and sugar and heat gently over a moderate heat. As soon as the water boils and all the butter has melted, remove from the heat. Add all the flour and beat hard with a wooden spoon until you have a smooth dough that comes away from the sides of the pan without sticking. Return the pan to the hob and continue to beat the dough over a low heat for a couple of minutes more. It will begin to thicken and dry.

Transfer the dough into a food processor or a mixing bowl and allow to cool for 5 minutes. Gradually add the eggs to the dough, a quarter at a time. Beat well after each addition. Continue beating until all the eggs have been incorporated and the dough is completely smooth.

Spoon the dough into a piping bag fitted with a 1 cm (½ in) plain nozzle. Pipe 2.5 cm (1 in) rounds of dough onto the trays leaving 2 cm (¾ in) gaps between each one. Bake for 10–15 minutes. When they are golden and firm remove from the oven and pierce the bottom of each profiterole with a wooden skewer. Cool on a wire rack with the holes facing upwards.

To make the sauce, place all the ingredients in a medium heatproof bowl over a pan of simmering water over a medium heat and stir until the chocolate has melted and the sugar has dissolved. Remove from the heat and keep warm.

To serve, carefully cut each profiterole in half. Scoop small balls of ice-cream and fill each choux bun with enough ice cream so you can see it peeking out of the sides when you sandwich the tops on. Drizzle the filled profiteroles with the warm chocolate sauce just before serving.

CARAMEL RICE PUDDING

Forget the British way of serving rice pudding with a dollop of jam and go for the French way of topping it with a drizzle of caramel sauce.

Makes 20

For the rice pudding

200 g (7 oz/1 cup) short-grain pudding rice

1 vanilla pod

900 ml (30 fl oz/3¾ cups) milk

75 g (2½ oz/¾cups) caster (superfine) sugar

pinch of salt

3 egg yolks

50 g (2 oz/¼ cup) butter

For the caramel sauce

150 g (5 oz/¾ cup) light soft brown sugar

200 ml (7 fl oz/scant 1 cup) double (heavy) cream

Bring a small saucepan of water to the boil, add the rice and cook it for 2 minutes. Strain and set aside.

Split the vanilla pod in half lengthways and scrape out the seeds. Place the pod and seeds in a large saucepan with the milk, sugar and salt and heat to a gentle simmer. Pour in the rice and stir well. Cover and simmer for 30–40 minutes, stirring occasionally to make sure the rice doesn't stick to the bottom of the pan. Remove from the heat when all the liquid is absorbed and the rice is tender.

Remove the vanilla pod. Add the egg yolks, return to the hob and heat gently for a few more minutes, stirring occasionally. Remove from the heat, stir in the butter and leave to cool.

To make the caramel sauce, heat the sugar in a saucepan over a medium heat. Keep an eye on it and stir frequently to ensure the sugar doesn't burn. When the sugar has melted remove the pan from the heat, leave to cool for about a minute, then slowly pour in the cream and stir until you have a smooth sauce.

Pour the rice pudding into individual small serving dishes. Serve the caramel sauce on the side for guests to add their own.

CHOUQUETTES

Pearl sugar has a very high melting point so the nibs survive baking and give these little buns an irresistible crunch.

Makes 50-60

120 ml (4 fl oz/½ cup) milk

100 g (3½ oz/scant ½ cup) butter, cubed

1 teaspoon salt

1 teaspoon sugar

140 g (4½ oz/1¼ cups) plain
(all-purpose) flour

5 eggs, beaten

icing (confectioner's) sugar, for dusting

100 g (3½ oz/½ cup) pearl sugar

Preheat the oven to 190°C (375°F/gas mark 5). Line 4 baking trays with baking paper.

Place the milk and 120 ml (4 fl oz/½ cup) water in a large heavy-based saucepan. Add the butter, salt and sugar and heat gently over a moderate heat. As soon as the water boils and all the butter has melted, remove from the heat.

Add all the flour at once, and beat hard with a wooden spoon until you have a smooth dough that comes away from the sides of the pan without sticking. Return the pan to the hob and continue to beat the dough over a low heat for a couple of minutes more. It will begin to thicken and dry.

Transfer the dough into a food processor or a mixing bowl (if making by hand) and allow to cool for 5 minutes. Gradually add the eggs to the dough, a quarter at a time. Beat well after each addition. Continue beating until all the eggs have been incorporated and the dough is completely smooth.

Spoon the dough into a piping bag fitted with a 1 cm (½ in) plain nozzle. Pipe 2.5 cm (1 in) rounds of dough onto the trays leaving 2 cm (¾ in) gaps between each one. Dust with icing sugar and leave for a minute before sprinkling with the nibbed sugar. Repeat with a second layer of icing sugar before baking for 10–12 minutes or until golden and crisp.

Transfer to a wire rack to cool. Best eaten on the day you make them.

CHOCOLATE TARTINES

These warm, chocolate-topped, golden toasts are a quick and easy, but sophisticated treat for when only chocolate will do! These are a firm favourite with kids and adults, and make a great afternoon snack.

Makes 12 small tartines

½ baguette, sliced into 1 cm (½ in) rounds

50 g (2 oz/⅓ cup) dark (bittersweet) chocolate (minimum 70% cocoa solids), broken into pieces

50 ml (2 fl oz/¼ cup) olive oil

sea salt

Preheat the grill to high and toast the baguette slices, on both sides, until just golden.

Place the chocolate in a medium, heatproof bowl over a pan of gently simmering water. Stir until melted.

Spread the melted chocolate over each slice of toast, drizzle with a little olive oil and top with a pinch of sea salt.

CRÊPES

*Serve in the classic way with a sprinkling of sugar
and a squeeze of lemon juice, plus a few fresh strawberries – when
they're in season – or a dollop of good-quality jam.*

*Makes 8 large or 24
small crêpes*

225 g (8 oz/1¾ cups) plain
    (all-purpose) flour

1 teaspoon sugar

pinch of salt

2 eggs, lightly beaten

550 ml (18½ fl oz/2¼ cups) milk,
    plus extra

1 teaspoon butter, melted

butter, for frying

To serve

caster sugar

1 lemon, cut into wedges

fresh strawberries or jam

Sift the flour into a large bowl and mix in the sugar and salt. Make a well in the centre and slowly pour in the eggs and beat together. Gradually add the milk and mix until you have a smooth batter. Don't over-mix as this will make rubbery crêpes. Stir in the melted butter. Cover and refrigerate for minimum of 30 minutes or even overnight.

When you are ready to cook the crêpes, stir the batter thoroughly and strain it to remove any lumps and add a little milk if it is too thick. Heat a 25 cm (10 in) crêpe pan or a deep non-stick frying pan and brush with a little butter. Pour a large spoonful of batter into the pan. Cook over moderate heat for about 1 minute then turn the crêpe over and cook on the other side for a minute or until lightly golden. Slide the crêpe out of the pan, then repeat to make as many as you can from the batter. Grease the pan lightly with butter in between each one. Stack the crêpes on a plate set over a pan of simmering water to keep them warm.

Sprinkle the crêpes with a little caster sugar, fold and serve with lemon wedges and fresh strawberries or jam.

MADELEINES

A traditional French cake with a distinctive pretty, scallop shape – perfect to serve for afternoon tea or morning coffee. Cover the batter and chill it in the refrigerator for up to 2 hours. This will ensure your madeleines have a nice rounded 'belly' once baked.

Makes 50–60

140 g (4½ oz/scant ⅔ cup) unsalted
   butter plus extra for greasing

125 g (4 oz/1 cup) self-raising (self-rising)
   flour plus extra for dusting

3 large eggs

140 g (4½ oz) caster (superfine) sugar

1 teaspoon clear honey

1 teaspoon finely grated lemon zest

1 teaspoon groundnut (peanut) oil

50 ml (2 fl oz) whole milk

Preheat the oven to 200°C (400°F/gas mark 6). Grease enough mini Madeleine tins to bake 50–60 cakes if you are making them in one batch, dust with flour, tap off any excess, then chill in the fridge.

Place the butter in a small saucepan, and melt gently over a medium heat, then set aside to cool.

In a large bowl whisk the eggs and the sugar together for 8–10 minutes until the mixture triples in volume and leaves a trail on the surface. Add the honey and the lemon zest and stir into the mixture.

Add the oil, sift the flour and fold in, together with the cooled butter and milk until it is all incorporated. Spoon the mixture into the chilled tins and leave to rest in the fridge for 5 minutes.

Bake for 5–10 minutes until firm to the touch and golden brown. Leave to stand for 1–2 minutes before removing from the tins. Transfer to a wire rack to cool. Madeleines are best eaten fresh on the day you make them.

SUGARED ROSE PETALS

Perfect for adding a very special finishing touch to a whole host of summery cakes and desserts. Sprinkle some over delicate, pale pink meringues... the possibilities are only limited by your imagination!

Makes about 24 candied petals

2 untreated and unsprayed roses

1 large egg white

125 g (4 oz/½ cup) caster (superfine) sugar

Preheat the oven to 30°C (90°F). Line a baking sheet with baking paper.

Gently detach the petals from the roses, discarding any that are damaged. Wash them in water and dry gently, one by one, with paper towels.

Lightly beat the egg white in a cup with a fork. Paint each petal on both sides with the egg whites using a small paintbrush. Sprinkle a small amount of sugar over the petals, turning them carefully to coat both sides, and place onto the baking sheet. Bake for 4 hours to crystallise them. Ensure that the temperature never goes higher than 30°C (90°F); if necessary open the oven door.

Store in an airtight container until ready to use.

FLOATING ISLANDS

The perfect light and airy dessert — soft meringues in a pool of frothy chilled vanilla crème anglaise topped with toasted almonds — fabulous!

Makes 8

For the meringues

5 egg whites

200 g (7 oz/scant 1 cup) caster (superfine) sugar

200 g (7 oz/1¾ cups) icing (confectioner's) sugar

400 ml (13½ fl oz/1¾ cups) milk, for poaching

For the crème anglaise

4 egg yolks

40 g (1½ oz) caster (superfine) sugar

200 ml (7 fl oz/scant 1 cup) double (thick) cream

200 ml (7 fl oz/scant 1 cup) whole milk

1 vanilla pod, split lengthways, deseeded, pods finely chopped

toasted almonds, to serve

Put the egg whites and a few tablespoons of the sugar into the bowl of food processor. Start whisking at low speed until the mixture begins to foam, then increase the speed to high and whisk until the foam thickens to form smooth, soft glossy peaks.

Add the remaining caster sugar, a little at a time, and continue whisking until the meringue stands in firm peaks. Finally, sift in the icing sugar and whisk briefly until it is incorporated.

Pour the milk for poaching into a large saucepan and bring it to a gentle simmer over a medium heat. Use two hot dessertspoons to shape the egg white mixture into 8 meringues. Poach 4 at a time, for 3–5 minutes, turning them in the milk so they poach evenly. Use a slotted spoon to remove from the milk and leave to dry on paper towels. Repeat to poach the remaining meringues.

For the crème anglaise, cream together the egg yolks and sugar in a large mixing bowl. In a heavy-based pan, combine the cream, vanilla pod and seeds, bring to the boil and simmer for 4–5 minutes. Remove from the heat and allow to cool for 30 seconds.

Pour the milk onto the egg and sugar mixture a little at a time so that the eggs do not cook, and whisk continuously until smooth and creamy. Return the mixture to the pan and place over a medium heat and stir for another 4–5 minutes or until the mixture has thickened. Strain the mixture through a sieve into a bowl, leave to cool then refrigerate until required.

To serve, fill 8 individual serving bowls with a pool of frothy vanilla crème anglaise and float the soft meringues on top. As a final flourish add some toasted almonds.

CRÈME BRÛLÉE

If you do not have enough pretty teaspoons to serve in this way, use some dessertspoons as well or pop the mixture into little ramekins instead.

Makes 30 teaspoons

3 vanilla pods

450 ml (15 fl oz/scant 2 cups) double (heavy) cream

450 ml (15 fl oz/scant 2 cups) whole milk

160 g (5 1/2 oz/¾ cup) caster (superfine) sugar

8 egg yolks

80 g (3 oz/⅓ cup) brown sugar

Split the vanilla pods in 2 lengthways, scrape out the seeds and place the pods and seeds in a large saucepan with the cream and milk. Bring just to the boil then remove from the heat and let the vanilla infuse for at least 30 minutes.

Preheat the oven to 150–160°C (300–320°F/gas mark 2–3).

Whisk together the sugar and egg yolks in a large mixing bowl. Remove the vanilla pod from the pan and pour the cream and milk over the egg mixture, whisking well until smooth.

Ladle the mixture into a 1 litre (34 fl oz) baking dish and carefully place in a roasting tin. Pour enough hot water into the tin to come half way up the side of the dish. Cook for 40 minutes or until just set.

Leave in the fridge for at least 2 hours, to set and cool completely.

Spoon the set crème brûlée onto pretty spoons, sprinkle each one with a little brown sugar and caramelise using a blowtorch. Alternatively, you can place them under the grill, but only if they are in a grill-proof ramekin. Serve immediately.

GRAND MARNIER TRUFFLES

Delectable, moreish, decadent, indulgent, truly luscious
and so simple to make – need I say more?

Makes 18 truffles

80 g (3 oz/⅓ cup) butter

150 ml (5 fl oz/⅔ cup) double
(thick) cream

300 g (10½ oz/2 cups) dark (bittersweet)
chocolate (minimum 70% cocoa solids),
very finely chopped

3 tablespoons Grand Marnier

100 g (3½ oz/¾ cup) unsweetened cocoa
powder, sieved

Heat the butter and cream in a medium saucepan over a gentle heat, until the butter melts. Add the chocolate, return to a low heat and stir until the chocolate melts.

Remove the pan from the heat and let it stand for 2–3 minutes. Add the Grand Marnier and set aside to cool, stirring occasionally to keep the butter incorporated. When cool, place the mixture in the fridge to firm up for about 30 minutes.

When it has cooled to the consistency of toothpaste, use a small spoon to scoop 18 balls of chocolate mixture. Work quickly as the mixture will melt quickly when it comes into contact with your warm hands.

Roll the balls lightly in cocoa powder until fully coated. Shake off any excess. Place the truffles in small paper cases to stop them sticking to each other. Store the truffles in an airtight container in the fridge. To serve, bring to room temperature for 30 minutes before eating.

PALMIERS

Named after palm leaves, these elegant, crisp little biscuits look great and are so easy to make using ready-made pastry. Add a little powdered cinnamon to the sugar for an alternative flavour.

Makes 28

flour, for dusting

375 g (13 oz) ready-made puff pastry

150 g (5 oz/⅔ cup) caster (superfine) sugar, plus 4 teaspoons

icing (confectioner's) sugar, for dusting

Preheat the oven to 180°C (350°F/gas mark 4) and line 4 baking trays with greaseproof paper.

Roll out the puff pastry on a floured surface until it is large enough to cut out 4 equal rectangles, each about 7.5 x 20 cm (3 x 8 in) and 5 mm (¼ in) thick.

Take one rectangle of pastry with the short side facing you and sprinkle lots of sugar on top of the pastry. Roll lightly with a rolling pin to press it into the dough; when you've pressed in as much sugar as the dough can hold, turn it over, add more sugar and lightly roll again. Repeat with the remaining pastry and sugar.

Roll each piece of pastry into a tight roll along the short end, without stretching, to the centre of the rectangle, then roll from the other end until the rolls meet in the centre. Repeat with the remaining sheets of sugared pastry. Wrap in plastic wrap and refrigerate for 20 minutes. Use a sharp knife to cut each roll into 7 x 1 cm (½ in) slices.

Roll the slices very lightly and lay them out on the prepared baking sheets so the flat, swirly surface is facing upwards. Dust with icing sugar and bake for 8–10 minutes until the pastry is crisp, caramelised and golden brown. Keep an eye on them for the last few minutes to make sure they do not burn. Cool on a wire rack before serving.

NATHALIE'S MELTING CHOCOLATE CAKES

These mini chocolate loaves make a change from the ubiquitous round cakes. Use mini paper baking cases or a silicon or metal mini loaf tray to bake these individual cakes.

Makes 12 mini loaves

200 g (7 oz/scant ¾ cup) butter, cubed

200 g (7 oz/1⅓ cups) dark (bittersweet) chocolate (minimum 70% cocoa solids), broken into pieces

200 g (7 oz/scant ¾ cups) caster (superfine) sugar

4 eggs

1 teaspoon plain (all-purpose) flour

Preheat the oven to 180°C (350°F/gas mark 4).

Place the butter and chocolate in a heatproof bowl over a pan of simmering water and stir until the chocolate has melted. Transfer to a large mixing bowl with the sugar, stir with a wooden spoon and leave to cool a little.

Add the eggs to the chocolate mixture, one at a time, stirring well after each addition. Finally, stir in the flour and mix well.

Pour the cake batter into 12 mini loaf cases and bake for 12–15 minutes until the centres are set but still a little wobbly. Turn the oven off but leave the cakes inside for another 10 minutes, then transfer to a wire rack to cool completely.

You can store these covered, in the fridge for up to 2–3 days. Take out 30 minutes before serving.

CHAMPAGNE GRANITA WITH STRAWBERRIES

This refreshingly tangy granita also tastes delicious served with minted melon, peaches or kiwi fruit. It makes the perfect finish to dinner in the garden at the end of a hot summer day.

Serves 8

For the granita

160 g (5½ oz/¾ cup) caster
   (superfine) sugar

zest of a lemon

750 ml (25 fl oz/3 cups) Champagne

For the strawberries

a few mint leaves

50 g (2 oz/⅓ cup) light brown soft sugar

zest and juice of 1 lemon

500 g (1 lb 2 oz/3⅓ cups) strawberries

Combine 250 ml (8½ fl oz/1 cup) water with the sugar and lemon zest in a heavy-based saucepan and heat gently until the sugar has completely dissolved. Increase the heat and bring to the boil, then simmer for 2 minutes. Remove from the heat and set aside for 10 minutes to infuse.

When completely cold, strain through a fine sieve and add the Champagne. Pour into a shallow container and freeze. Every few hours take the mixture out of the freezer and beat it lightly with a fork to mix the frozen crystals into the liquid. By the time it has frozen, the texture should be granular with large icy crystals.

Meanwhile, roll the mint leaves into tubes and slice them thinly into ribbons. In a large bowl, whisk together the brown sugar and lemon juice and zest. Gently add the strawberries and mint ribbons. Toss together until the strawberries are well coated. Cover and chill for up to 4 hours to allow the flavours to blend.

To serve, put a spoonful of strawberries into small serving glasses or cups and top with the Champagne granita.

CHOCOLATE ÉCLAIRS

The French pâtisserie classic, crisp choux pasty fingers filled with a rich chocolate and vanilla crème and topped with a sweet, sticky icing.

Makes 20

For the choux pastry
(see Ice Cream Profiteroles recipe on page 73)

For the chocolate crème pâtissière filling
500 ml (17 fl oz/generous 2 cups) whole milk
1 teaspoon vanilla extract
6 medium egg yolks
75g (2½ oz/⅓ cup) caster (superfine) sugar
20g (¾ oz/¼ cup) plain (all-purpose) flour
2 heaped tablespoons cornflour (cornstarch)
30 g (1 oz/¼cup) dark (bittersweet)
    chocolate (minimum 70% cocoa solids),
    broken into pieces
1 heaped tablespoon unsweetened
    cocoa powder

For the glaze
200 g (7 oz/scant 1 cup) fondant icing
1 tablespoon unsweetened cocoa powder
1–2 tsp water

Preheat the oven to 190°C (375°F/gas mark 5). Line 2 baking trays with baking paper.

To make the choux pastry follow the Ice Cream Profiteroles recipe on page 73, up to the point of piping the mixture out.

Spoon the dough into a piping bag fitted with a 1 cm (½ in) plain nozzle. Pipe the dough about 7.5 cm (3 in) in length onto the trays leaving gaps between each one. Bake for 10–15 minutes. When they are golden and firm remove from the oven and pierce the bottom of each éclair with a wooden skewer. Cool on a wire rack with the holes facing upwards.

To make the crème pâtissiere filling, combine the milk and vanilla in a heavy-based saucepan and bring to the boil. Simmer very gently for about 5 minutes and then take off the heat and cool. In a large bowl, whisk together the egg yolks, sugar, flour and cornflour. Pour in the milk, whisking continuously and bring back to the boil over a medium heat for 1 minute. Pour the mixture into a bowl and leave to cool.

Melt the chocolate in a heatproof bowl over a pan of simmering water then pour the melted chocolate into the crème pâtissière. Add the cocoa powder and whisk to a smooth consistency. Spoon the filling into a piping bag fitted with a 5 mm (¼ in) nozzle and carefully fill each éclair.

To make the glaze, place the fondant icing in a small pan and gently melt the fondant over a low heat. Stir in the cocoa powder and 1–2 teaspoons water until evenly combined. Using the back of a spoon spread the glaze over each éclair and place on a wire rack. Allow to set in the fridge until ready to serve.

ABOUT THE AUTHOR

Nathalie Benezet comes from a family of French restaurateurs. For most of her childhood she grew up in the Parisian restaurants, bars and cafés managed by her parents and grandparents. From them she inherited her passion and love for the business.

During the past decade she has developed and managed several restaurants and retail outlets in the catering and hospitality industry. Nathalie shows passion for everything food-related, and her contribution to the food industry earned her a 'Grand Prix des Jeunes Créateurs du Commerce' in France.

Today Nathalie lives between Paris and London.

INDEX

Le Petit Paris

First published in 2013 by Hardie Grant Books

Hardie Grant Books (UK)
Dudley House, North Suite
34–35 Southampton Street
London WC2E 7HF
www.hardiegrant.co.uk

Hardie Grant Books (Australia)
Ground Floor, Building 1
658 Church Street
Melbourne, VIC 3121
www.hardiegrant.com.au

British Library Cataloguing-in-Publication Data. A catalogue record
for this book is available from the British Library.

ISBN 978-1-74270-596-5

Commissioning Editor: Kate Pollard
Desk Editor: Kajal Mistry
Photography by Jacqui Melville
Food Styling by Nicole Herft
Cover and Internal Design by Rebecca Guyatt
Colour Reproduction by p2d

Printed and bound in China by 1010

10 9 8 7 6 5 4 3 2 1